Elephant Walk

Alison Hawes
Illustrated by Rory Tyger

RIGBY

The big elephants
come up the hill.

Up the hill
come the little elephants.

5

The big elephants
come down the hill.

Down the hill
come the little elephants.

The big elephants
come over the bridge.

Over the bridge
come the little elephants.

13

Down comes the bridge!

Down come **all** the elephants!